P9-CRZ-589

What Stinks?

BY
MARILYN SINGER

DARBY CREEK PUBLISHING

PHOTO CREDITS

4: fulmar © Steffen Foerster/iStockphoto; rafflesia © Duncan Butchart; ginkgo seed © Steven J. Baskauf; ailanthus © Les Mehrhoff/IPANE. **6:** doggie doo © Robert Bredvad; **7:** making friends © Brandon Clark/iStockphoto; adult Komodo dragon © Tom Marvin/iStockphoto. **8:** otter © Norma Cornes/Dreamstime.com; dog poop © Lee Pettet/iStockphoto; horse manure © Nicola Stratford/iStockphoto; bat guano, muskrat scat, red fox scat, raccoon scat © Acorn Naturalists/AcornNaturalists.com; red fox © Lisa Haggblom/USFWS photo; muskrat © Dave Menke/USFWS photo; bat © Adam Booth/iStockphoto. **9:** dog paw © Ivar Teunissen/iStockphoto. **10:** young Komodo dragon © Peter Chen/iStockphoto. **11:** European fieldfare, hoopoe © Frank Tiegler; anopheles mosquito: This material is taken from the "Food and Environmental Hygiene Department's Web site" and is reproduced under a license from the Government of the Hong Kong Special Administrative Region. All rights reserved. **12:** dog making his mark © Jason Pacheco/iStockphoto; rhino spray © Mike Powles/Oxford Scientific/photolibrary; red fox © Nicola Gavin/iStockphoto. **13:** ring-tailed lemur © Josef Hlasek. **14:** pelican © Jeremy Voisey/iStockphoto; skua © Joe Lindsay/iStockphoto. **15:** fulmar © Ashok Rodrigues/iStockphoto; robin © Lee Karney/USFWS photo; pelican © Gary M. Stolz/NPS photo. **16:** hoatzins © Ra Khalil/Dreamstime.com; stinky cat breath © David Elfstrom/iStockphoto. **17:** acorn worm © Mark Terasaki; earthworm © Kristen Eckstein/iStockphoto; ribbon worm © Mary Jo Adams; eel © Asther Lau Choon Siew/Dreamstime.com; *Ircinia* sponge © Greg McFall/NOAA Gray's Reef National Sanctuary; tube sponge © Dennis Sabo/Dreamstime.com. **18:** *Ircinia* sponge in the Caribbean © Jay Adkins/iStockphoto; opossum © Steve Geer/iStockphoto; panda © Wang Sanjun/Dreamstime.com; Tasmanian devil © Steve Lovegrove/Dreamstime.com; groundhog © Steve McWilliam/Dreamstime.com; greater moon rat © Konstans Wells; hedgehog © Ole Geisselbrecht/iStockphoto. **19:** Tasmanian devil in distress © Dave Watts/Naturepl.com; garter snake © Erik Hendrickson/NPS photo; stinkpot turtle © Mark B. Watson; mink frog © S. Mierzykowski/USFWS photo; green tree frog © Willie Manalo/Dreamstime.com. **20:** stinkbug © Roger Chalkley/University of Cincinnati. **21:** raven © Gary M. Stolz/USFWS photo; grasshopper mouse/NPS photo. **22:** bombardier beetle © Dr. Thomas Eisner/Visuals Unlimited; argiope spider © Donna Carlson/iStockphoto. **23:** ladybug © Scott Bauer/USDA ARS Photo Unit; lubber grasshopper © Bill Waller; swallowtail caterpillar's osmeterium © www.larvalbug.com. **24:** *Danaus chrysippus* © Miss Tingting Mo/www.bjbug.com; *Hypolimnas misippus* © Miss Tingting Mo/www.bjbug.com; Devil's Rider walking stick © M.C. Thomas/Division of Plant Industry, Florida Department of Agriculture and Consumer Services. **25:** earwig © Roger Chalkley/University of Cincinnati. **26:** dog tick © Chartchai Meesangnin/iStockphoto; daddy longlegs © Joe Kazimierczyk/www.joekaz.net. **27:** whip scorpion © Richard Seaman; African giant millipede © Ralton Bentley/iStockphoto. **28:** hooded skunk © Mary Root; hog-nosed skunk © R.D. Lord/Mammal Images Library of the American Society of Mammalogists; spotted skunk © California Living Museum. **29:** skunk preparing to spray © Thomas Kitchin/Tom Stack & Associates. **31:** musk turtle © Mark B. Watson. **32:** musk deer © Brent Huffman/Ultimate Ungulate Pages; musk duck © Paul Gullan/Viridans Images; musk turtle © Mark B. Watson; muskrat © Steve Geer/iStockphoto; musk melon © Charles Schurch Lewallen. **33:** civet © Nigel Dennis, SA Tourism Image Library; Bactrian camels © Valerie Crafter/iStockphoto; billy goat © Scott Bauer/USDA ARS Photo Unit. **34:** bull elephant © Brian Kelly/Dreamstime.com. **35:** javelina © Barry Nielsen/NPS photo. **36:** rafflesia blossom © Duncan Butchart; moth © Dawn Hudson/Dreamstime.com. **37:** starfish flower © Karri Egger/iStockphoto; titan arum/work of United States Federal Government. **38:** titan arum/work of United States Federal Government; flies pollinating the dead horse arum © Marc Gibernau. **39:** pelican flower © Wayne Boucher/cambridge2000.com; Bradford pear blossoms © Kelly Pollack/iStockphoto; pawpaw fruit © Leah-Anne Thompson/Dreamstime.com. **40:** bat © Phil Date/Dreamstime.com; kapok blossom © Angela Bell/iStockphoto; field of baobab trees © Muriel Lasure/Dreamstime.com. **41:** Namaqua rock mouse pollinates a *Protea humiflora* © Colin Paterson-Jones. **42:** inside of a durian © Christopher Rayan/SXC; durian © Phil Date/iStockphoto. **43:** orangutan enjoying a durian © Neil Lucas/Naturepl.com. **44:** white spruce/NPS photo; tree-of-heaven © Les Mehrhoff/IPANE; white stopper © Ken Cook/Plant Creations, Inc.; black stinkwood © Duncan Butchart; gidgee © Len Webb/Ecological Images Collection. **45:** ailanthus grows along the roadside © Les Mehrhoff/IPANE; ailanthus seedlings © Les Mehrhoff/IPANE. **46:** white stopper © Ken Cook/Plant Creations, Inc.; white spruce needles/USFWS photo; poison hemlock © Steven J. Baskauf. **47:** boxwood © Marc Marien/Dreamstime.com; stink grass © Mike Haddock/Kansas State University. **48:** mushroom on a tree stump © Jim Jurica/iStockphoto; stinkhorn © P. Super/NPS photo; flies feasting on a gooey stinkhorn © Scott Camazine. **49:** grapes with bunch rot © Mike Ellis/Ohio Agricultural Research and Development Center, Department of Plant Pathology. **50:** flowering garlic © Joanne Harris/Dreamstime.com. **51:** leeks © Lynn Watson/iStockphoto. **53:** rue/NPS photo. **54:** garlic cloves © David Guyer/iStockphoto. **56:** boy sniffing pine © Anna Chelnokova/iStockphoto; girl sniffing rose © Monique Harris/iStockphoto; mad scientist © Maartje van Caspel/iStockphoto. All other photos from royalty-free stock sources are not credited.

Cataloging-in-Publication

Singer, Marilyn.
What stinks? / Marilyn Singer.
     p. ; cm.
ISBN-13: 978-1-58196-035-8
ISBN-10: 1-58196-035-2
Includes bibliographical references.—Summary: Why do some animals, insects, plants, and trees smell the way they do? Find out how they use smells to mark their territories, defend themselves, communicate, or even attract a mate. 1. Animal chemical ecology—Juvenile literature. 2. Plant chemical ecology—Juvenile literature. 3. Odors—Juvenile literature. 4. Smell—Juvenile literature. [1. Animal chemical ecology. 2. Plant chemical ecology. 3. Odors. 4. Smell.]
I. Title. II. Author.
QL751.5 .S564 2006
[591.5/1] dc22
OCLC: 60942018

Published by Darby Creek Publishing
7858 Industrial Parkway
Plain City, OH 43064
www.darbycreekpublishing.com

Printed in the United States of America

1 2 3 4 5 6 7 8 9 10

What's Inside

Introduction:
What Stinks?

What Do These Things Have in Common?

They STINK! They don't all smell the same way or for the same reason, but they all smell *bad*—at least to most of us humans.

Why do some plants and animals stink? What is the purpose of a bad smell? Can something that smells nasty to you smell good to another creature? Can something that smells nasty be *good* for you?

You're about to go on a smelly adventure to find out not only what stinks, but also *why*. So, hold your nose and keep reading!

Do You Smell Something?

What we call smell is our response to chemicals called *odorants*, carried by the air around us. We breathe in or swallow the odorant, which is then brought to *receptor cells* high up in our noses. These cells carry a signal to the olfactory area in our brain that declares, "Smell!" We learn to recognize the odor and also to be aware of many things, such as whether we're near food, danger, a person we do or don't like, or a familiar place.

No two people smell odor the same way. Women generally have a better sense of smell than men, and— because our senses deteriorate as we age—kids have a better sense of smell than adults.

lemur

fulmar

rafflesia

swallowtail caterpillar

ginkgo seed

ailanthus

Some cultures don't think the sense of smell is very important—but other cultures do. In India, a traditional friendly greeting is to smell someone's head. In some Arab countries, breathing on people when talking to them is a sign of goodwill. To avoid doing so means the speaker doesn't want to be friends. The Ongee people of the Andaman Islands define everything by smell. They greet each other with "How is your nose?" If a person answers, "I'm heavy with odor," the greeter must remove some of it by inhaling deeply. If the person has a lack of odor energy, the greeter supplies some by blowing on him or her.

bug antennae (above) &
hairy bug feet (below)

We all have a different idea of what smells bad or good. In Ethiopia, for example, some people find the scent of cows lovely. In Mali, the Dogon people like the smell of onions. In the U.S., people often dislike natural body odor, so we spend a lot of money on deodorants and perfumes to cover it up.

The average person has about five or six million receptor cells in each nostril and can recognize up to 10,000 odors. That sounds like a lot. But a rabbit has 100 million of these cells, and a dog has 220 million. Think of all the odors they can smell!

bird nostrils

Mammals use their noses to smell things, but other creatures use different means. Fish and birds have no noses, but they do have nostrils. Insects have neither noses nor nostrils— they detect odors with their antennae (feelers), and some bugs also can smell things with their feet. Tiny hairs with nerve cells cover these body parts. The odorants contact the hairs and reach the nerve cells' receptors. Insects cannot detect as many odors as people can, but they are able to smell much smaller amounts of them and over greater distances.

Some scientists now think that to repel insects effectively, we need to block their sense of smell. Experts are working on chemicals to prevent mosquitoes from detecting humans, fruit flies from sensing rotting fruit, and other pests from finding foods they like to eat.

KIDS HAVE A BETTER SENSE OF SMELL THAN ADULTS.

Much Ado about Doo

doggie doo

SOME ANIMALS' FECES IS SO VALUABLE THAT IT'S COLLECTED AND EVEN SOLD.

To most people, "poop" and "stink" are synonymous—they mean the same thing. Excrement is mainly water. The rest of it is stuff we can't digest, such as fiber, fats, salts, protein, mucus, cells from the intestines, and live and dead bacteria. The smell is caused by compounds and gases produced by some of these bacteria as they break down our food. It varies according to what a creature eats or drinks.

Everything that eats has to get rid of waste materials. Therefore, animals need to poop. We humans don't usually think our poop is worth much, so we flush it away. But we find some other animals' feces so valuable that we collect and even sell it—as fertilizer. Manure from farm and zoo animals such as horses, cows, and elephants and guano from bats and seabirds may make fields and gardens stink, but they also nourish plants and help the soil stay moist.

Animals don't give fertilizer much thought. For them, poop has different, but important, uses.

manure (above) & pelican poop (below)

Hey, Are You Harry?

Lots of mammals and reptiles smell or even taste feces to identify which friends, relatives, enemies, and strangers have recently visited their neighborhoods. A dog sniffing another dog's doo-doo can tell if Mom, good old pal Harry, or that rottweiler from down the block was around—and even how recently. A Komodo dragon, the world's largest

making friends

lizard, will take as long as ten minutes to sample another Komodo dragon's fecal pellets to find out who passed by. Why is this useful information? It can tell the sniffer whether it's safe to go ahead or if it's time to retreat. It can also help the lizard find a mate. The pellets may even reveal what food the visitor ate and whether there's good hunting in the neighborhood.

adult Komodo dragon

NAME FIVE THINGS THAT CAN BE DONE WITH POOP:

1) Flush it down the toilet.
2) Use it to grow corn.
3) Put it on a rock near your home.
4) Sniff it to see if it's your pal Harry's.
5) Roll in it!

I Live Here—and I Have the Poop to Prove It!

Within a neighborhood, each animal has its territory. Some animals are more concerned with protecting their turf than others. Territorial birds may use delightful songs to declare, "This is my place!" But some mammals—including muskrats, otters, raccoons, foxes, and bobcats—use their poop. They leave their scats as "keep out!" signs on rocks, logs, and

otter

prominent places where other muskrats, otters, raccoons, foxes, or bobcats can easily see—and smell—them. Foxes coat their scats with a bacteria-rich fluid from their anal glands to make the poop smell even stronger. There are other ways of using dung to mark territory, as well.

WHO LEFT THIS HERE?

Match the scat with its animal owner.

a

b

c

d

e

f

red fox

horse

raccoon

dog

muskrat

bat

ANSWERS: a) dog; b) bat; c) muskrat; d) horse; e) red fox; f) raccoon

Who has the smelliest feet?

a) a dog

b) a rhino

c) you

What Did You Step in?

A critter with stinky feet is the African hyena. It scrapes the ground, leaving scent from glands between its toes to mark territory. It also has anal glands under its bushy tail that it uses to paste a strong-smelling white substance on tall stalks of grass. Both males and females scent-mark to establish territory. Hyenas are not in the dog family, but, like canines, they also roll in poop, most likely to disguise their natural odor.

The hyena, you, and Fido could probably not beat a rhino's feet for big-time stink. Rhinoceroses are mostly solitary animals with poor eyesight but a good sense of smell. Each needs a territory large enough to supply the plants it eats. The two places rhinos do share as a group are the water hole, where they drink and bathe, and the toilet. All rhinos in a particular neighborhood defecate in the same big heap. Then each rhino purposely drags its hind feet through the poop. When it leaves, the rhino tracks that odor through its range as a kind of invisible, but smelly fence.

spotted hyena

rhinoceros at the water hole

PUPPY PAWS AND PEOPLE FEET

ALL HUMAN FEET STINK.

Your pooch sweats through his paws, so his feet may be a bit smelly, but the odor is not usually that strong or unpleasant to people. Your feet are another story. All human feet smell because people (along with many other animals) produce chemicals called *pheromones* that give each of us a unique odor and help to attract mates. But these pheromones are subtle, not easy to detect. Really stinky feet are caused by *microbes*—tiny plants and animals that grow on your skin, especially when it's dirty and sweaty. The same is true of our armpits and other body parts.

Washing your feet will eliminate some microbes and their bad smell. But nothing can get rid of all of them.

Poop Perfume

Any wolf or dog can tell you that one of its favorite uses for poop—many kinds of poop, in fact— is to wear it like perfume. Why do dogs roll in poop? Some scientists say it's to disguise their own odor so enemies won't attack them. Others say it's to advertise themselves to mates and friends. And still other people believe the main reason dogs roll in poop is because it's just good, dirty fun!

young Komodo dragon

poop-rolling dog

Young Komodo dragons are also poop-rollers. The adult lizards are fierce *carnivores*—they eat many kinds of animals, including their own youngsters. They are also efficient eaters and devour almost all of their prey, including the guts. However, they dislike the taste of poop, so before they eat the guts, they shake out the feces. The young Komodos then roll in the doo to make themselves taste bad to their parents. For baby Komodos, poop is protection from Mom and Dad!

Stay Away or I'll Poop on Your Head!

Komodo dragon youngsters are not the only creatures to use poop in self-defense. Some birds do, too—but in a much more aggressive way.

Hoopoe and woodhoopoe chicks, found in the woodlands of Europe and Africa, squirt liquid poop at intruders' faces. The moms defend their babies by spraying the intruders with a foul-smelling oil from a preen gland at the base of their tails. In addition, hoopoes are known for never cleaning their nests, so they reek of excrement, a stench that probably keeps predatory mammals, such as cats, far away.

European field-fares also poop on enemies. If a magpie or other predator approaches a fieldfare colony, the fieldfares fly into the air and bomb the intruder with feces. These attacks destroy the enemy bird's plumage and can even kill the trespasser. Some predators, such as small falcons, have discovered that it's safe to raise their own young in field-fare colonies. In exchange, the falcons leave the fieldfare chicks alone.

European fieldfare

hoopoe

MOSQUITO BAIT

You may find smelly feet gross, but researchers have recently discovered that one creature loves the aroma—the anopheles mosquito that causes malaria, a dangerous disease. Scientists hope that they will be able to create that odor artificially and use it to make better mosquito traps.

anopheles mosquito

To Pee or Not to Pee

dog making his mark

rhino spray

Poop is not the only substance used for marking territory. Urine will also do the trick. In addition to making poop-scented trails, male rhinos claim their turf by spraying pee on grass, trees, and posts. They can squirt their urine nine to twelve feet behind them. The stench covers a wide area and lasts day after day after smelly day. It also advertises that the rhino is available as a mate.

USES FOR URINE

Fox urine is not only used by foxes. Some people bottle it and sprinkle it in the garden to repel mice, rabbits, rats, squirrels, woodchucks, chipmunks, and other small animals that foxes eat. These creatures will think a fox is around, and they'll stay away.

In addition, fox, coyote, wolf, mountain lion, and bobcat pee are used by dog trainers to keep puppies from urinating in various areas of their yards and lawns. Pups don't want to mess with predators either—even if the predators aren't really there.

red fox

Red foxes, too, use urine to mark territory, especially good hunting grounds and empty storage areas. Foxes bury food they've caught. If they smell their own urine near an area that they've already emptied of food, they know not to bother to dig up the spot.

Many animals spray their turf with a mixture of scent and urine. One whole family of mammals does so—*mustelids*, which include weasels, stoats, minks, otters, polecats, wolverines, badgers, and ferrets, among others. Mustelids have large anal scent glands. They also sometimes spray when they're frightened, as do foxes and other animals.

But the most famous sprayers are probably cats—all types of cats, from a small Siamese to a huge Bengal tiger. Feline females that are ready to mate and unneutered males sometimes spray, too. But that familiar, foul cat odor most often comes from unneutered toms squirting pee and scent around to declare, "I'm me and I *own* this place!"

Stink Fight!

Poop, pee, and spray are all stinky ways to *mark* territory. But some animals use bad smells to *defend* territory. One of those creatures is the lemur.

Like apes, monkeys, and people, lemurs are *primates*—animals that can grasp things with their fingers and opposable thumbs (thumbs that can move to touch any of the other fingers on the same hand). Ring-tailed lemurs live in small troops on Madagascar and nearby islands. Unlike monkeys, lemurs cannot hang by their long tails. They spend most of their time on the ground.

ring-tailed lemur

Each troop has its turf and will defend this territory from other troops. Instead of hitting or biting, lemurs protect this territory by waging stink fights. These bloodless battles mean that no lemurs get hurt, a win-win situation even for the losers.

How does a troop of lemurs stage a stink fight? If you were a lemur, here's what you'd do:

1. Check out your wrists. See the scent glands there? The ones with the small spurs? Rub those spurs into another pair of scent glands—the ones on your upper arms.

2. Now comb those spurs through your tail. Comb them good! Get that aroma all over it.

3. Here comes that enemy troop. Get ready, get set—get 'em out of here! Lift that tail high! Stand on your hands if you have to. Chitter, growl, make plenty of noise. But whatever you do, keep waving that tail over your head like a smelly flag!

4. That's it! You won! They're gone. Now settle down and take a nap. You and your tail have earned it!

I Did It in Self-Defense!

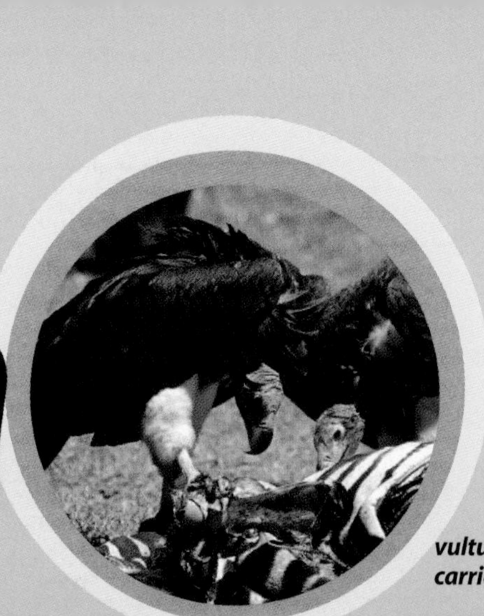

vultures eating carrion

FISH-EATING PELICANS WILL USE THEIR OWN VOMIT AS A MEANS OF SELF-DEFENSE.

Ask any animal what's the most important thing to defend and it will tell—no, it will *show* you: *itself*. Territory is important all right, but it doesn't mean much if you're not alive to claim it.

To protect themselves, animals have many kinds of defenses. Lions, wolves, bears, and other predators have formidable teeth and claws. Eagles and hawks have sharp beaks and talons. Armadillos have armor. Tarantulas have venom. Elephants have size. But other creatures have to make do with repulsive odors.

And what could be more repulsive than vomit? It's not surprising that some animals barf in self-defense, especially some otherwise helpless birds.

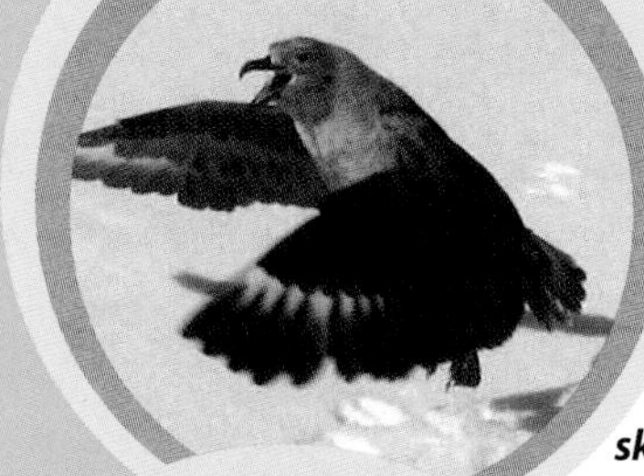

skua

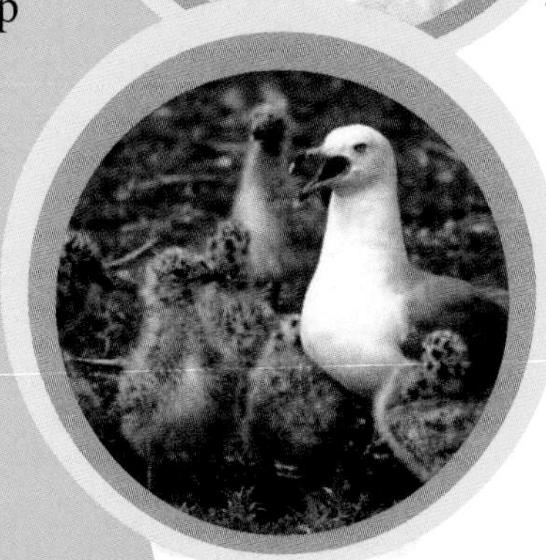

fulmar with chicks

Blowing Chunks!

Vultures eat carrion—dead and rotting animal flesh. When threatened, these birds are known for throwing up their recent smelly breakfast, lunch, or dinner, preferably right in the face of an attacker. Fish-eating pelicans will also puke in self-defense.

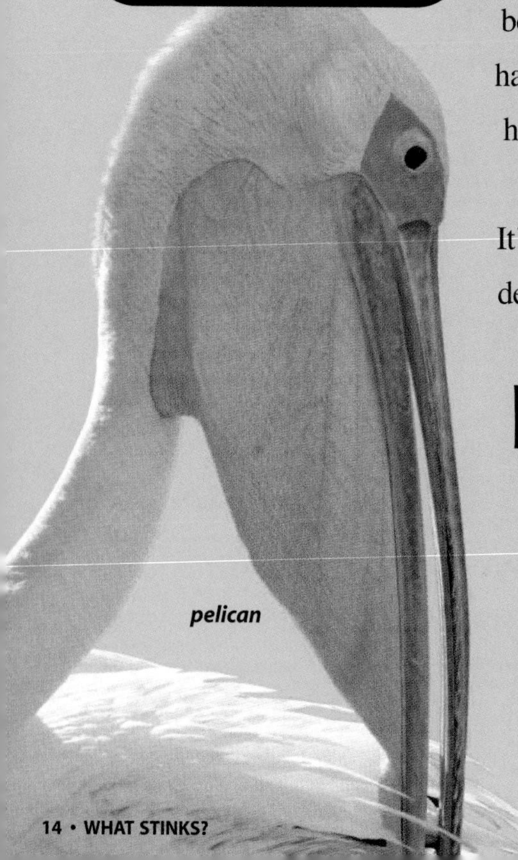

pelican

One of the most interesting barfing birds is the fulmar. The fulmar is part of a family known as the *tubenoses*, seabirds whose nostrils are enclosed in tubes on their large, hooked bills. "Fulmar" means "foul gull," and that's a good description of one of the world's stinkiest birds.

When an intruder such as a cat or a skua—a type of predatory bird—approaches a fulmar on its nest, the bird spits up a malodorous stomach oil. This nasty stuff is disgusting to mammals, which have a keen sense of smell, and also to other birds because it clings to and damages their feathers.

Even tiny fulmar chicks can spit this odoriferous oil. Studies have shown that a four-day-old chick can eject the oil a distance of one foot. An adult bird can expel its spit up to five feet—and these birds can throw up three or more times in a row.

It's important for fulmar chicks to be able to defend themselves because they are left alone for many hours while their parents are hunting for fish out at sea. Until they learn to recognize their parents, young fulmars will vomit at them, too. Fortunately for the adults, they are somehow immune to the bad effects of the oil, though scientists as yet don't know how. In fact, the adults use small amounts of it for preening. The oil also seems to be nutritious—fulmar parents feed it to their young and to each other when they are courting.

In addition to the oil, all species of fulmars have a disagreeable body odor. Even their eggs smell bad, so they and the birds themselves are unappetizing. This foul gull has certainly made the most of smell as a defense.

WHICH OF THESE BIRDS IS MOST LIKELY TO BARF IN YOUR FACE?

vulture

robin

pelican

fulmar

hawk

swan

Stink Bird of the Amazon

The smelliest—and weirdest—bird in the world is probably the hoatzin (pronounced *WAT-zin*), known by local residents as the "stink bird." Found near the Amazon, the hoatzin eats mainly leaves and has an enlarged *crop*—storage area in the chest—to help digest them. It is the only bird that has such a digestive system, which resembles a cow's. The leaves ferment inside the crop, making the whole bird smell like manure. Parents feed their chicks regurgitated leaves, so the youngsters stink, too. Although people and many other hunters avoid eating these birds, some predators will try to catch them.

hoatzins

Hoatzin chicks have another and even stranger defense. They are born with two claws on each wing, making them look like tiny pterodactyls. If a predator comes near them, they dive into the water. Once the danger has passed, they use their claws to climb back to their nests.

HAVE YOU EVER HEARD OF *MOUTHWASH???*

Pelicans and other fish-eaters have bad breath. So do many other animals. Bad breath—known as *halitosis*—comes from the decay of food particles in the mouth. Particularly stinky food causes smellier breath. But only humans tend to be offended by this smell. Other animals are not bothered by it. They may even like it. They sniff each other's mouths to find out who they are and what they've been eating.

stinky cat breath

Saliva is the key to getting rid of bad breath. It washes away the food particles and bacteria. The reason our breath smells worse in the morning is because when we sleep, we don't produce much saliva, allowing bacteria to grow. Eating stimulates saliva production and brushing our teeth rids our mouths of the particles and odor. Some folks also use mouthwash. If you smelled a pelican's breath, you might wish it used mouthwash, too. But the pelican wouldn't agree.

Stinkers, Stinkers Everywhere

Vomit and poop are only two types of stinky protection. All over the world are creatures that spray, ooze, or foam obnoxious fluids or gas in self-defense.

By and Under the Sea . . .

Worms are known for being slippery. But some worms are also known for their smell. Several species of acorn worms produce a bromide compound in their tails. This compound smells like iodine and may protect the worms from germs—and from predators. The creatures burrow headfirst in the mud or sand and raise their tails to poop. Predators will sometimes bite off the tails, but the odor probably repels many of them. Shrimp that do manage to eat these worms also end up smelling like iodine, which may in turn protect them.

WHICH ONE IS THE STINKER?

acorn worm

earthworm

ribbon worm

eel

Ircinia *sponge*

tube sponge

Ircinia *sponge in the Caribbean*

In the world's oceans, including the chilly Antarctic, there are eight hundred species of ribbon worms. They average five to ten feet in length, but some are as long as sixty feet. They produce lots of pungent mucus, which turns off predators. Scientists who handle the worms find that their hands will stink for a long time.

In the Caribbean, sponges of the *Ircinia* group repel predators with a substance that makes them smell like garlic. No wonder these sponges have names such as "stinker sponge."

WHICH ONE IS THE STINKER?

opossum panda

Tasmanian devil or groundhog

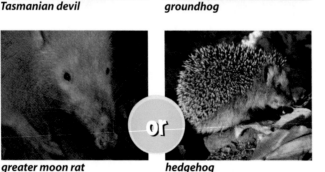

greater moon rat or hedgehog

On Land . . .

You've already met the mustelids. Now greet the opossum. This mammal—the only American marsupial—defends itself by playing dead. When it is frightened, its body stiffens, its tongue rolls out of its mouth, and it drools. In addition, an opossum may ooze nasty-smelling green mucus from its rear end, ensuring that no predator will eat it.

The Tasmanian devil doesn't look anything like the cartoon character Taz. It is another marsupial, and it's found only on the Australian island of Tasmania. This carnivore got its name from its big teeth, scary gape, and the eerie sounds it makes. A whole group of Tasmanian devils will screech and scream as they devour a carcass. These noises help the animals establish dominance—the louder and fiercer a devil can sound, the higher its rank. And what about its smell? That's devilish, too. If a Tasmanian devil feels stressed, it opens its mouth in a wide yawn and emits a nasty odor from its scent glands.

The greater moon rat, the world's largest insectivore, also gives off a foul stench. Found in Borneo and related to the non-stinky hedgehog, the moon rat has coarse bristles instead of spines. Its defense is to give off a rotten garlic smell from its anal glands. It repels even persistent predators, such as snakes. The moon rat is highly immune to snake venom, but snakes are apparently not immune to its odor.

Tasmanian devil in distress

Reeking Reptiles and Amphibians

Most snakes can produce a pungent scent when disturbed, and studies have shown that the females may produce a stinkier one than the males. This may be a natural way to defend the eggs or live young they are carrying. The garter snake in particular is well known for this chemical defense, probably because this common reptile has bombed more folks than any other kind of snake. Pick up a garter snake and, P.U.! Once it gets used to being handled, however, the garter snake generally stops releasing its defensive odor.

Another reptile, the small stinkpot or musk turtle of the eastern U.S., also produces a foul smell when captured. The mink frog, an amphibian in the northern U.S., secretes a substance that has been described as smelling like the stinky mink. What does a mink smell like? Think rotten onions.

WHICH ONE IS THE STINKER?

garter snake

gecko

stinkpot turtle

box turtle

mink frog

green tree frog

Fuggy Bugs

Insects and their relatives are probably the largest group of animals to use odor as protection. They need strong defenses because they are prey to so many kinds of animals. Take the stinkbug—please! This shield-shaped insect and its cousins live throughout North America and other parts of the world, so chances are good that you may run into one in your garden. Some stinkbugs are helpful because they eat weeds and the eggs of harmful insects, but others are crop pests, devouring fruits and vegetables.

stinkbug

We call all insects *bugs,* but, in fact, *true* bugs are a special order of insects called *Heteroptera.* Like all true bugs, the stinkbug has beak-like sucking mouthparts and forewings that are half-hard and half-soft. And true to its name, it stinks! When disturbed, it can emit a nasty-smelling juice from glands in its thorax. You can easily get a stinkbug to ooze by gently squeezing its sides. But be warned—the smell will linger on your hands, and, if you're allergic to the juice, you may get a rash. So it's best to leave this insect alone.

NOT ALL INSECTS ARE CLASSIFIED AS *TRUE* BUGS.

elytra

Funky Beetles

Members of the genus *Eleodes* are also sometimes called stinkbugs, but they are not true bugs. They are beetles, which means that their forewings are two hard sheaths, called the *elytra*, which

beetle

darkling beetle in defensive position

raven

grasshopper mouse

raccoon

protect the soft hind wings. In the U.S., *Eleodes,* or darkling beetles, as they're commonly named, are found in western deserts where they wander in search of plant material to eat. During the summer, these insects are nocturnal. During the winter, they're diurnal, or active in the daytime.

On some beetles, the elytra can separate and open. But a darkling beetle's elytra are fused. That means it can't escape predators by flying away—because it can't fly! So it has developed another defense. When it is threatened—in particular by birds, rodents, or raccoons—the beetle turns into an acrobat. It does a headstand and then, depending on the species, it oozes or squirts a foul-smelling brown or reddish-brown oily substance from its rear end. The larger species of darkling beetles can spray several times, and each burst may reach as far as twenty inches. The irritating oil burns and causes temporary blindness if it gets into an intruder's eyes. That gives the beetle time to scuttle quickly away. Grasshopper mice have learned how to avoid this oil by grabbing the beetles, shoving their rear ends into the ground, and eating their heads first.

Bombs Away!

The bombardier beetle can't fly either, so this amazing insect also relies on a toxic spray. However, the bombardier's ammo is unique—not only does it smell bad, but it is also boiling hot! How can a beetle store hot, irritating spray inside its body without dying? Each of its two glands has two separate chambers, and each chamber contains a chemical.

bombardier beetle

When the beetle is attacked, the chemicals are released from the first chamber into the second, or *reaction chamber*, where the two chemicals mix. The mixture gives off heat and pressure until it is forced out of the bombardier's rear end with a *POP!* that we humans can actually hear. Like a gunner, the beetle can spray this mixture in single shots or in rapid-fire bursts, and in all directions—up, down, and even over its back.

YOU CAN STINK, BUT YOU CAN'T HIDE

The bombardier is one sharp-shooting stinker! But it does have a powerful enemy—the argiope spider, which also preys on stinkbugs. Some types of spiders catch prey in the sticky strands of their webs, bite them with their venomous fangs, and then wrap them up to feed on later. Argiopes have a different strategy. After they catch an insect in their web, they wrap it first, and then they bite it. They are so skilled in this process that they can wrap insects that have chemical defenses before they have a chance to spray or ooze. Argiopes succeed at feasting on stinkers where other spiders fail.

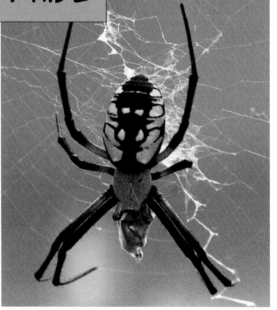

argiope spider

Color Me Nasty

Sometimes a creature not only has the ability to stink—it wants to warn the world that it can! That's just what the beloved and familiar ladybug does. When it's pestered, the ladybug oozes unpleasant-smelling orange oil from glands in its legs. But unlike the plain-colored bombardier, the ladybug gives fair warning that it smells and tastes rotten—through its colors. Its bright red-orange and black dots announce that a ladybug is toxic. This kind of warning pattern is called *aposematic*. It proclaims, "Eat me and you'll be sorry. REALLY sorry!"

ladybug

Aposematic species are frequently black, red, yellow, or orange, or they are marked with various combinations of black, red, yellow, and orange. The distinctively colored lubber grasshopper is also aposematic. This big, bumbling insect, found in

lubber grasshopper

the southern U.S., can't fly, but it is never in any hurry to get out of the way of a predator.

It doesn't need to rush—it has several powerful defenses it can use instead. First it flashes its warning colors. If that doesn't work, it lets out a scary hiss. If the hunter is still foolish enough to attack, the lubber brings out its big weapon—vile-smelling foam that makes most birds violently ill when they eat it. Once a bird tastes a lubber, it doesn't want a second helping.

swallowtail caterpillar's osmeterium raised

Swallowtail caterpillars have a fascinating aposematic organ called an *osmeterium*. It is bright orange and Y-shaped, and it springs out from a segment right behind the caterpillar's head. The sudden appearance of this organ is enough to startle off some predators. The nasty smell is enough to chase away most of the rest of them.

You may be wondering how a bird or other hunter learns to stay away from a smelly, poisonous creature. After all, animals are not born knowing that ladybugs, lubbers, and swallowtails are poisonous. Remember when you were little and you put something gross in your mouth? You spit it out in a hurry, right? Soon, you began to recognize that object and never again tried to eat it.

Young creatures do the same thing. They learn to associate colors with bad taste and smell and avoid prey with those markings. This means that some animals from every aposematic species will die—but their sacrifice prevents thousands of cousins from being eaten.

Some species even mimic poisonous ones—they have aposematic colors, but they're fakes. They're not poisonous at all! Their enemies don't know that, though, and they don't risk their taste buds or stomachs.

The *Danaus chrysippus* is poisonous to its prey. The *Hypolimnas misippus* is not, but it mimics the other butterfly's colors in order to stay safe.

Danaus chrysippus
(poisonous)

Hypolimnas misippus
(not poisonous)

Sticks with a Stench

The opposite of aposematic coloration is camouflage. It is a device animals use to blend into their environment—and it is also a great defense. Stick insects have excellent camouflage: They resemble twigs. They can lie motionless for hours and are undetected by predators.

If their camouflage fails to work, some species, such as the Devil's Rider walking stick *(Anisomorpha buprestoides)* use another defense. They emit a foul chemical spray that is irritating to the nose and eyes.

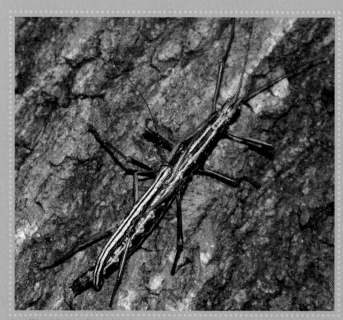

Devil's Rider walking stick

The spray contains a chemical compound similar to the one in catnip—a strong-smelling herb that drives some cats crazy. Studies have shown that the compound in catnip protects the plant from insects, just as the walking stick's spray drives away birds, ants, and other predators.

earwig

Like walking sticks, earwigs are outdoor insects. They sometimes crawl into your house (but never into your ears). If disturbed, they squirt a foul-smelling liquid. They can also pinch with the pincers at the end of their abdomen, but they can't seriously hurt you. Females have straight pincers. Males have curved ones, which they use to battle other males and to clasp females during mating. Both use their pincers to catch prey—other insects and spiders.

Home, Smelly Home

Some insects are social—they group together. The whole colony produces a smell called an *aggregation pheromone*. This odor declares, "Party at my house!" Each individual in the group gives off this pheromone, but people can't detect the odor until a bunch of these individuals get together in one place.

a cockroach colony

One of the best known and nastiest aggregation pheromones is given off by that disliked pest, the cockroach. We can't stand the stench, but cockroaches like it. The odor, along with their feces, makes a place smell like home—*their* home, that is. Different species of cockroaches produce different odors. Among the stinkiest is the hissing cockroach, which grows up to three inches long and makes a loud, scary hiss to frighten predators. The hissing cockroach has been a star in horror movies for years! Despite its odor and sound, it is a harmless creature. Some people even keep it as a pet.

Arachnids' Awful Aromas

dog tick

Insects have six legs and three body sections: the head, the thorax, and the abdomen. Arachnids, such as spiders, scorpions, ticks, mites, and daddy longlegs, have eight legs and two body sections: the anterior, or *cephalothorax*, and the posterior, or abdomen.

Most spiders and their arachnid relatives don't stink. They have fangs and venom for both hunting and defense. But the harvestman, or daddy longlegs, does. These arachnids have venom, and they use it to catch insects to eat, but they can't bite people or other large animals because their jaws don't open wide enough. Perhaps that's why they need extra protection.

daddy longlegs

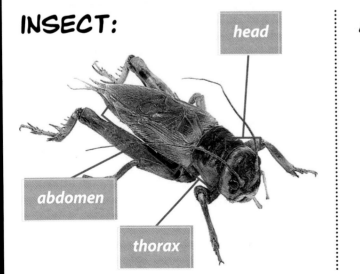

INSECT:

head

abdomen

thorax

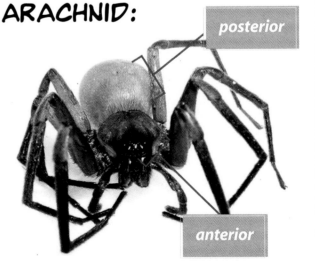

ARACHNID:

posterior

anterior

When a daddy longlegs is attacked, it oozes a smelly fluid and then uses its legs to smear this chemical on the attacker. Scientists found that this leg-brushing technique is highly effective in getting rid of predators, particularly ants.

A Stinker, Not a Stinger

Scorpions are arachnids with claw-like pincers and poisonous stingers at the end of their tail-like abdomens. Residents of the southwestern U.S. deserts, whip scorpions do not have stingers. Instead, they have long whip-like "tails." They defend themselves by spraying a chemical mixture that smells like strong vinegar, giving these animals their common name: *vinegaroons*. Whip scorpions

whip scorpion

can defend themselves against many kinds of predators, including grasshopper mice, which are known to eat scorpions. The whip scorpions' success at repelling hunters helps explain why they've been around for a long, long time—300,000 or more years, according to fossil records.

MILLIPEDES AND MURDER

African giant millipede

Like spiders, millipedes are related to insects. These arthropods are known for their segmented bodies and many legs. But predators recognize some of them for their smell as well. African giant millipedes, among others, release a yellowish secretion from pores on the sides of their bodies. They give off a strong scent similar to the smell of bitter almonds, an odor made famous in murder mysteries. It is associated with one of the world's deadliest poisons—hydrogen cyanide. In fact, that's exactly what the millipede is releasing.

A millipede can produce enough cyanide to kill a mouse, but it doesn't release that much at one time. Toads and other animals sometimes manage to eat these insects by swallowing quickly and not giving the millipede time to squeeze its body segments in order to fire the cyanide.

The Ultimate Sprayer

hooded skunk

hog-nosed skunk

spotted skunk

Close-up on Skunks

Want to annoy your brother or sister? Just call him or her a *mephitid*. What's a mephitid? Only the most famous smelly animal in the Americas: the skunk! Although other mammals certainly stink, no other mammal is as well-known for its foul self-defense.

All skunks are in the *Mephitidae* family—a Latin word for "bad odors." In fact, the familiar striped skunk's Latin name is *Mephitis mephitis*. Translation: "Stinky stinky." Several skunk species are common: striped, spotted, hooded, and hog-nosed among them. The striped skunk is the most widespread throughout the U.S. These solitary, omnivorous animals hunt at dusk and dawn and help rid fields, farms, and woods of vermin and other pests.

SKUNKS WILL SPRAY ONLY AS A LAST RESORT.

striped skunk

All skunks have super-large anal glands that can spray a noxious, oily, yellow liquid as far as fifteen to twenty feet with great accuracy. The main ingredient in this oil is a sulfur compound—the same stuff that makes rotten eggs smell rotten. It can cause temporary blindness if it gets in a predator's eyes.

Because of this potent weapon (and their poor eyesight), skunks tend to walk around slowly and fearlessly, their bold black-and-white markings advertising the fact that they smell bad. But the truth is they spray only as a last resort. A skunk will first try to run away from a predator. If that's impossible, it may hiss, growl, stomp its front feet, and shuffle backwards. If the predator still won't back down, the skunk will then spray. Different skunk species spray in different ways. Most predators hightail it out of there when a skunk begins its display.

All varieties of skunks have enemies. One is the great horned owl, which doesn't have a good sense of smell but can swoop down and grab a skunk before it has time to spray.

Skunks will not spray near their dens or at other skunks, even if they have a fight. Mephitids apparently don't like their own stink either!

HOW TO SPRAY LIKE A SKUNK

You're a striped, hooded, or hog-nosed skunk, and you've hissed, growled, and stomped your feet, each in your unique way. But that dumb intruder is still there. What do you do?

1) If you're a striped skunk: Now it's time to turn around and twist your body into a *U* so that both your head and tail face the enemy.

2) If you're a hooded or hog-nosed skunk: Just turn your back to that intruder and lift your tail.

3) Keep that bushy tail up. Stand your ground.

4) Contract the sphincter muscles in your rear end. Let 'em have it!

If you're a spotted skunk, and the hissing, growling, and stomping didn't work for you either, it's time to go acrobatic.

1) Put your front feet on the ground and do a handstand.

2) Keep your tail up, too. Be cute, but deadly.

3) Contract those sphincters and fire away—directly over your head!

skunk preparing to spray

What will eliminate the odor? Tomato juice, right? Wrong! Tomato juice only *seems* to work because, after smelling strong skunk spray for a while, humans experience *olfactory fatigue*. That means our sense of smell gets so tired we can no longer detect a particular odor, even a nasty one. When this happens, we smell the tomato juice instead. But has it really eliminated the skunky perfume? The answer is no. Anyone who comes on the scene will tell you that you or your dog still reek of skunk—even if you can't smell it.

What *does* eliminate skunk perfume? Try this:

1) Combine 1 quart of 3% hydrogen peroxide, 1/4 cup of baking soda, and 1 teaspoon of liquid detergent.

2) Bathe your pet with this mixture.

3) After five minutes, rinse with water. Repeat if necessary.

> *Warning:* Do not store this mixture in a closed container— it releases oxygen gas that can break it. It may also bleach a dog's fur. As for clothes, towels, or other materials that are "skunky," wash those in a washing machine with one cup of liquid bleach per gallon of water.

What a Gas!

Not every spray is used to mark territory or as self-defense. Some spray just . . . happens. *Flatus*—the nasty-smelling gas we pass—is actually a mixture of gases we breathe in, ones created from the food we eat, and tiny particles of feces produced in the intestines. The odor comes from butyric acid and sulfur compounds that occur when proteins are digested—the same odor found in poop. The noise happens because the flatus is forced out by pressure.

Most mammals, birds, fish, and even insects can fart. In some cultures, farting is rude, embarrassing, or funny. In others, it is perfectly acceptable. It's not healthy to hold in gas, so farting is a good thing—although perhaps not in a crowded elevator or your classroom.

It "Musk" Be Love!

musk ox

musk turtle

Musk is a pungent odor that has given its name and fragrance to a variety of plants and animals: musk turtle (stinkpot), musk duck, musk ox, muskrat, musk thistle, musk rose, musk melon, and musk mallow, just to name a few. Some of these plants and animals smell nasty. For example, male musk oxen have a gland under their eyes that they rub on branches of bushes and trees during mating season to attract females. Others are rather sweet (the musk rose—ahh!). In addition, the bad odor from skunks, mustelids, snakes, and other creatures is also called musk. Confused? Let's look into the mystery of musk.

The Real Musk-ateer

Real musk comes from a gland in the abdomen of the male musk deer. This Asian deer uses the reddish-brown secretion to mark territory and to attract females of the species during breeding season.

REAL MUSK COMES FROM A GLAND INSIDE A MALE DEER.

musk rose

By itself, musk is too strong for most people to wear as perfume—although people from some cultures have used it undiluted. But when musk is mixed with alcohol and other oils, it has a luscious smell and helps the oils retain their sweet or spicy fragrance. That's why for centuries musk has been used in perfumes.

The bad news is that many musk deer have died just so people can smell good. Hunters slaughtered the deer in droves and removed their glands. Now most perfumers use artificial musk. However, the genuine stuff is still prized—not only for fragrance, but also for medicine. Even though musk deer are protected, poachers still kill them. Because of poaching and habitat destruction, this gentle species is endangered, even extinct in some of its range, and several wildlife organizations are working to save it.

male musk deer

MATCH THE PICTURE WITH THE NAME:

musk turtle
musk duck

musk ox
musk rose

musk mallow
musk melon

musk thistle
muskrat

ANSWERS: a) musk duck; b) musk rose; c) musk thistle; d) musk melon; e) musk turtle; f) muskrat; g) musk ox; h) musk mallow

Muskmaking Civets

The *civet*, a carnivorous Asian animal related to the mongoose, produces a stinky substance similar to real musk. It is secreted from the civet's anal glands and is used for the same purposes as the musk deer's. Both males and females can make this musk, and, like musk deer, civets were frequently killed for it. Then perfumers figured out how to keep the civets in small cages and scrape out their musk glands every fourteen to twenty days—a cruel and painful process for the animals. Fortunately, the manufacturing of artificial musk is causing this practice to die out.

civet

Love Me, Love My Smell

In musk deer and civets, the musk mixes with urine so the animals can spray it on bushes, trees, rocks, and other spots. Many other animals, such as the already-mentioned cats, use a urine and glandular mixture to attract mates. Billy goats pee all over themselves, including their faces, during mating season. Male Bactrian camels use their tails to splash their urine over their rear humps. During courtship, a male porcupine urinates on a female. If she smacks him, bites, shakes off the urine, or runs away, she is rejecting him. If she doesn't object to the pee, he's her choice for a mate.

Another even larger creature uses both urine and a facial secretion to attract a partner. Can you name it?

Bactrian camels

billy goat

mother elephant and her calf

How Does an Elephant Say, "Choose Me"?

a) It gives flowers.

b) It bakes cookies.

c) It whispers sweet-nothings.

d) It jumps up and down.

e) It oozes and pees.

bull elephant

MALE ELEPHANTS CAN BECOME HOSTILE WHILE IN A STATE OF MUSTH.

If you guessed **e**, you've gotten the hang of this book. That's right—when bull elephants want to show how attractive they are, they ooze fluid and urinate.

Periodically males go into a state called *musth*. During this state, their hormone levels rise and they become hostile—ready to fight other males to prove they are hot-shots. They make rumbling noises, secrete sticky liquid from the temporal glands located between their eyes and ears, and pee constantly. The secretion is pungent, and some elephant handlers have described it as having the odor of gunpowder. Musth urine is much stronger-smelling than non-musth urine. In addition, males flap their ears a lot, possibly to waft the odors toward other elephants.

These odors do several things. They warn other males about how powerful a bull is, which probably prevents battles because underdogs steer clear of top dogs. The odors also show females how powerful a bull is, too—and that he's likely to father strong babies. Musth does not necessarily coincide with mating, though. The female breeding cycle, called *estrus*, may occur at different times from musth. But studies seem to show that when the cow elephants are ready to mate, they will choose high-ranking bulls that they found attractive when the males were in their musth state. No wonder they say an elephant never forgets!

I'm in the Mood for Moda

Young male elephants go into a type of musth called *moda*. Instead of smelling bad, their secretions are sweet, like honey or flowers. These smells tell bulls and cows that the youngsters are inexperienced males—they pose no threat to the older ones.

Each elephant's scent, whether in or out of musth, whether male or female, is unique. Elephants don't need a telephone to communicate over long distances or a business card to say who's who—all they need are their trunks to take a good, long sniff.

JAVELINAS: A GAMY GAME

You may smell a *javelina*, (pronounced *ha-vay-lee-na*), or collared peccary, long before you see it. Its skunky smell is detectable from hundreds of feet away. This pig-like critter—found in southwestern U.S. deserts and Central and South America—has a powerful musk gland on its rump. A javelina rubs the substance from this gland on rocks and other objects to mark territory and smears it on other javelinas to establish a herd smell. Each herd has its own signature stench, which gets even stronger when the group gets excited. Since javelinas have poor vision, they locate buddies by scent rather than sight. Odor keeps each herd safely together—and different herds safely apart.

javelina

Foul Flora

The Rancid Rafflesia

What weighs as much as a miniature poodle and smells as bad as rotten dog food? Would you believe it's a *flower*? The rafflesia is the world's largest flower. When it's in full bloom, it can weigh up to fifteen pounds and be a yard wide. Found on rain forest floors in Indonesia, Borneo, and Sumatra, it is a parasite that lives off the roots of a vine related to the grapevine. Having no roots, stems, leaves, or chlorophyll, the rafflesia gets its food from that plant.

rafflesia blossom

The rafflesia takes nine months to reach full size. Then it bursts out like a big, orange cabbage and expands into a blossom as much as three feet wide and up to fifteen pounds in weight. Flowering for just four to six days, it fills the air with a stench like carrion, which has earned it the name "stinking corpse lily."

Why would any flower smell like that? The answer has to do with *pollination*.

Two, Four, Six, Eight— Now's the Time to Pollinate!

In order to reproduce, most flowers need to be pollinated. For flowers to make fruit and seeds, pollen from the male parts needs to reach the female parts. Some plants can pollinate themselves. Others must be pollinated by wind, water, or animals.

If a flower smells yummy during the day, chances are that it is pollinated by butterflies, bees, wasps, certain beetles, or other insects that are attracted to sweet odors. Pollen clings to them and is deposited on other blossoms. Pale or white flowers that are fragrant at night usually attract moths. Dull-colored, odorless plants are often wind-pollinated. Some bright, odorless blooms may be pollinated by birds, such as hummingbirds, which have a poor sense of smell. The birds go to drink nectar, and the pollen sticks to their feathers or beaks.

bee covered with pollen

hummingbird

Colorful but unscented flowers also appeal to bees, wasps, and butterflies, which look for blossoms of particular colors and shapes and not just scent. And if a flower smells—and sometimes even looks—bad, it lures flies, carrion beetles, or other critters that love the putrid odor of rotten meat or fish.

WHICH OF THESE FLOWERS SHOULD YOU *NEVER* GIVE MOM ON MOTHER'S DAY?

rose

iris

rafflesia

delphinium

titan arum

cattleya orchid

skunk cabbage

starfish flower

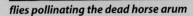
flies pollinating the dead horse arum

titan arum

The Carrion Crew

Rafflesias are pollinated by those kinds of flies and beetles. The insects check out the malodorous plants to see if they're tasty and end up carrying the pollen from one flower to another. Studies have shown that the insects cannot tell the difference between the odors given off by carrion flowers and those emitted by actual carrion. They will even lay their eggs on the plants, expecting that their young will get a good meal. For the flowers, it's a successful strategy; for the baby flies and beetles, it's starvation.

Some carrion flowers trap the insects inside until pollination is complete. The dead horse arum (*Helicodiceros muscivorus*), found on small islands in the Mediterranean, lures blowflies carrying pollen from other dead horse arums down its funnel-like sheath. The flies pollinate the female flowers at the bottom of the sheath. They cannot escape because they are blocked by disks of dense, stiff hairs. Once the male flowers above these hairs release pollen, the hairs wilt and the flies leave, carrying the pollen to other arums.

SOME CARRION FLOWERS TRAP INSECTS INSIDE FOR SUCCESSFUL POLLINATION.

Other carrion flowers include the starfish flower (*Stapelia gigantea*); the pelican flower (*Aristolochia grandiflora*); the exotic, twelve-foot-tall titan arum (*Amorphophallus titanum*), the odor of which has made people faint; and the familiar wetland plant, skunk cabbage (*Symplocarpus foetidus*). One of the earliest wildflowers to bloom, a skunk cabbage can generate and maintain enough heat—a temperature of 70 degrees—to melt the snow around it and spread its aroma through the whole woods. Flies appreciate not only the odor, but also the plant's warmth. To some people, the plant is nasty; however, to this author, it smells like spring!

pelican flower

skunk cabbage

PRETTY PUTRID PETALS

Some smelly flowers are not as dramatic as the carrion flowers. The white blossoms of Bradford pear trees, often found on city streets, are as delicate as ballerinas—but they smell like a locker room. Some hawthorn trees also have lovely and fetid blooms. Pawpaws produce delicious fruit from slightly stinky blossoms. From the small, rank, red blooms of carob trees come pods that are used as a chocolate substitute, found in many health-food store products. Flies or beetles pollinate all of these trees.

pawpaw fruit

Bradford pear blossoms

Going Batty!

Flies and beetles aren't the only creatures attracted to smelly flowers. Many plants are pollinated by bats. What odors do bats prefer? Some like the smell of rotting fruit. And some like the musty aroma of fellow bats.

In Africa, the baobab tree (*Adansonia digitata)* produces gorgeous blossoms that reek rather like these flying mammals. Because bats are nocturnal, the flowers open at night and are pale in color so the bats can see (and smell) them more easily. While they are eating the flowers' nectar, the pollen sticks to the bats' fur or mouths. As they fly from bloom to bloom, they transfer it.

bat

kapok blossom

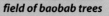

field of baobab trees

The baobab is a magnificent and important plant. Animals live in its branches. People use all of it—the bark for cloth and rope, the leaves for medicine, the fruit for food—and sometimes even take shelter inside its huge trunk.

Another important relative of the baobab is the silk cotton tree (*Ceiba pentandra*). This tree's fruits produce *kapok*—a fluffy material once widely used in lifejackets, sleeping bags, quilts, mattresses, and pillows because it is buoyant and warm. In many places the wood is still used to make canoes. Like the baobab, the kapok has malodorous flowers that attract bats. In some places, bats appear to be the plant's *only* pollinator and seed disperser. Eliminate the bats, and you eliminate the tree—one of many good reasons to protect these mammals.

Baobab and kapok blossoms, like carrion flowers, certainly smell great to their animal pollinators, but there's a good chance Mom won't like them. So when it comes to Mother's Day, it's best to stick with roses.

A Nose for Nectar—and Pollen

The clasping-leaf sugarbush (*Protea amplexicaulis*) is a type of *protea*, an evergreen shrub or tree native to Africa. The blossoms of this bush grow close to the ground, and, according to several sniffers, the flowers stink like dirty, wet socks or strong yeast. But the odor isn't aimed at attracting flies or bats. Like several other proteas, the clasping-leaf sugarbush is designed to interest rodents, such as the Namaqua rock mouse and the Cape spiny mouse, that find the odor appealing and the low-growing blooms convenient. The mice stick their faces into the flowers to lick their abundant nectar and come away covered with pollen, which they transfer to other blossoms.

A Namaqua rock mouse pollinates a Protea humiflora.

In South Africa, the African lily (*Massonia depressa*) is pollinated by several species of nocturnal gerbils. The sturdy flowers, which lie on the ground, attract these rodents with their yeasty odor and gobs of jelly-like nectar. Some scientists believe that the gooeyness of the nectar discourages flies, but encourages the gerbils, which find it easy to lap up.

More Plants with P.U. Power

Beware of Falling Fruit!

If you lived in Southeast Asia, you would probably know the *durian* is known as the King of the Fruits. Loaded with vitamins and minerals, it is famous for its sweet, delicious, pudding-like flesh—and its horrendous smell. One diner described it as "French custard passed through a sewer." In some places, taxis, buses, ferries, subways, airports, and hotels won't allow passengers to carry durians with them.

It's dangerous to stand under a durian tree when the hard, spiny fruits ripen. The rind and spines protect the durians until their seeds are fully developed. Then the fruits fall to the ground. Some of them can weigh as much as thirteen pounds. You wouldn't want one to land on your head!

Humans who like to eat this stinky food are attracted by the smell, which tells them the

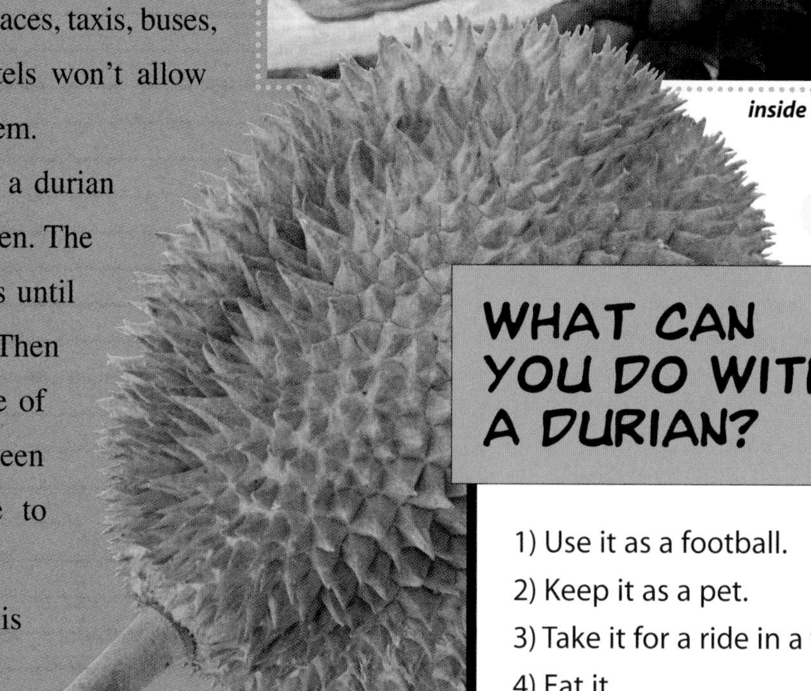

inside of a durian

durian

WHAT CAN YOU DO WITH A DURIAN?

1) Use it as a football.
2) Keep it as a pet.
3) Take it for a ride in a taxi.
4) Eat it.

durian is ripe. Elephants, tigers, pigs, deer, tapirs, rhinoceroses, monkeys, orangutans, bears, and other animals are also drawn to the odor. Some of these creatures, such as elephants, can smash open the fruits with their feet. But the durians often crack open when they fall so that other animals can also get to the pulp. After they've eaten their fill, the diners excrete the big seeds, dispersing them all over the forests to grow into new durian trees.

CERTAIN ANIMALS ARE ATTRACTED TO THE STINK OF A RIPE DURIAN.

orangutan enjoying a durian

Stinko Ginkgo!

fan-leaved ginkgo

Every fall, all over Park Slope, Brooklyn, where I live, the streets smell like dog poop. Of course, some of the odor *is* caused by dog poop. But most of it comes from the smashed seeds of the ginkgo trees—the odor that inspired this book.

The fan-leaved ginkgo is an elegant, ancient species—so ancient that it existed in the Jurassic period, when dinosaurs walked the earth. In fact, dinosaurs may have been responsible for spreading the seeds of this tree. Ginkgoes have no flowers, so they can't produce true fruits. But their seeds are surrounded by fleshy pulp that makes them resemble small apricots. When the seeds are ripe, the pulp produces a nasty odor that probably attracted prehistoric animal munchers—possibly sauropods that ate the pulp and excreted the seeds. Nowadays, Asian cuisine and medicine feature these seeds—minus the stinky pulp. They are mild and nutritious. If a dinosaur were around today, it might sing the praises of ginkgoes. But now you'll just have to take a *Homo sapiens*'s word for it.

A Stink Tree Grows in Brooklyn
(and Australia, Borneo, Canada, South Africa . . .)

Almost every continent has a smelly tree or two. This map shows where some of the biggest stinkers can be found.

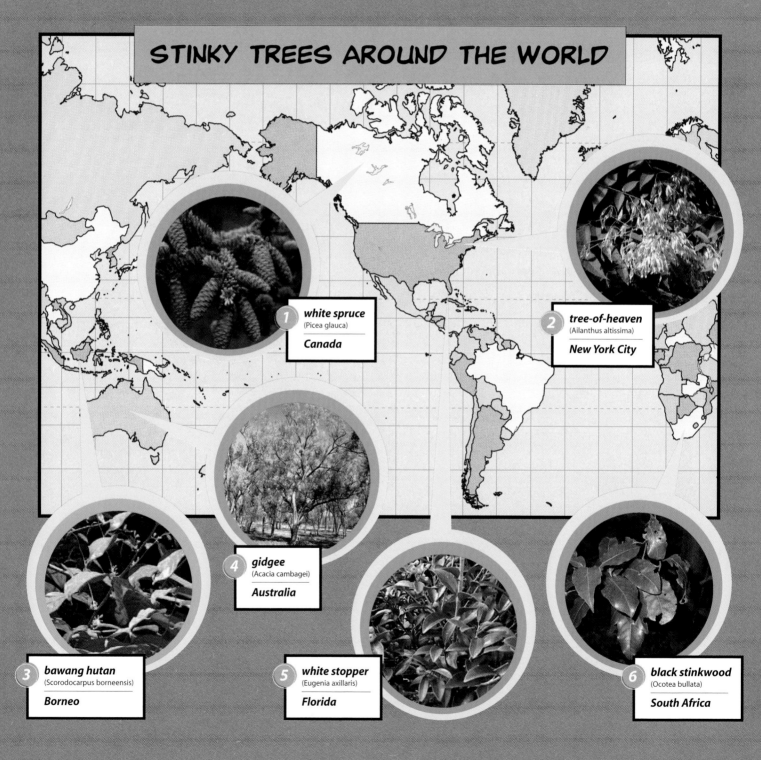

STINKY TREES AROUND THE WORLD

1 **white spruce**
(Picea glauca)
Canada

2 **tree-of-heaven**
(Ailanthus altissima)
New York City

3 **bawang hutan**
(Scorodocarpus borneensis)
Borneo

4 **gidgee**
(Acacia cambagei)
Australia

5 **white stopper**
(Eugenia axillaris)
Florida

6 **black stinkwood**
(Ocotea bullata)
South Africa

Stinking to High Heaven

Ailanthus altissima. It's called the "tree-of-heaven"—and you could probably smell it all the way up there. The flowers stink, and so do all the other parts of the plant. Native to China, this handsome tree was brought to Europe and then to the U.S. in the eighteenth century. It has been planted in many cities because it grows quickly, can thrive in poor soil, and resists pollution.

Unfortunately, it also invades areas easily and has been called a "weed tree" in many places. A single plant can produce more than 300,000 seeds in a single year. They are carried by the wind and reproduce in vacant lots, parks, gardens, cracks in the side-walk, rooftops—almost anywhere! In addition, the "tree-of-heaven" seems to be *allelopathic*, meaning it cuts down on the competition for space by producing toxins that prevent other plants from growing nearby.

Brooklynites have a love-hate relationship with the ailanthus. This weed tree is the title plant in Betty Smith's famous 1943 novel *A Tree Grows in Brooklyn*. Today this New York borough is still home to these stinkers—in fact, the yard next door to my house boasts a whole smelly grove of them.

ailanthus grows along the roadside (above) & scattered seedlings (below)

What is the purpose of the ailanthus's aroma? The same as a stinkbug's or a skunk's—self-defense. Mammals, birds, insects, and other creatures are repelled by the odor and won't eat the plant.

AILANTHUS IS ONE TOXIC AND COMPETITIVE PLANT!

Don't Eat the Leaves (or Anything Else)

Quite a few trees have unpleasant aromas in self-defense. Some, like the white stopper found in Florida, have skunky-smelling leaves. Others, such as the white spruce, a popular Christmas tree native to Canada, have needles that, when crushed, give off an odor similar to cat urine. When rain is coming, all parts of an Australian gidgee or stinking wattle (*Acacia cambagei*) smell like onions. Born in Borneo, the bawang hutan means "forest onion," which describes the odor of its wood. The black stinkwood tree (*Ocotea bullata*) also has an unpleasant odor when it is freshly cut, but that hasn't prevented people from over-harvesting this plant for its fine timber.

white spruce needles

white stopper

Smoking Can Kill You!

Poison hemlock (*Conium maculatum*) is another fetid plant. When its leaves are bruised, they emit a strong "mousey" odor. The smell repels animals. That's a good thing, because this is one weed that can kill. All parts of the plant are toxic. If the plant is burned, even the smoke is poisonous.

"Leaf" Me Alone!

Trees aren't the only leafy plants that smell bad to prevent being eaten. There are also stinky shrubs, herbs, and flowering plants, including varieties of elderberries, currants, salvias, and knotweed. Even some varieties of the pretty iris (*Iris foetidissima*) and peony (*Paeonia brownii*) are stinkers.

elderberries

Some of these are marketed today as "deer-resistant" plants. One of these, a smelly shrub called boxwood (*Buxus sempervirans*), has long been used as a low-growing evergreen hedge in herb and knot gardens. Some people like the bitter scent of the leaves. Other folks hate it. Queen Anne, who ruled England from 1702 to 1714, loathed the aroma and had all of the bushes removed from the palace grounds at Hampton Court.

boxwood

Gardeners are always eager to find plants that repel dogs, cats, bunnies, and other critters that eat—or urinate on—them. Some gardeners are singing the praises of *Coleus canina,* nicknamed the "pee-off plant." It has fleshy leaves and small blue flowers, and it gives off an odor that animals can't stand. Apparently people can only smell it if they touch the plant. So listen to this coleus when it says, "Look, but don't touch!"

Grass with Glands?

Most grasses don't smell bad. Stink grass (*Eragrostis cilianensis*) does. Most grasses also don't have glands. Stink grass does. These glands produce its odor. Introduced from Europe, this plant is an invasive species, widely spread in the U.S. throughout waste areas, along roadsides, and in fields. Because of its stench, cattle and horses avoid the grass—and that is probably its purpose. Like the ailanthus, the smell of stink grass may be a by-product of allelopathy as well. Stink grass is also known as "love grass." What on earth could love *this* smelly invader?

stink grass

Stinky Fungus among Us

Quick! What color do you associate with plants? If you answered "green," give yourself a lettuce leaf for lunch. But can you name a whole group of organisms that grow in or on the earth but for the most part *aren't* green? If you answered "fungi," give yourself a whole salad!

Fungi are not plants. They rule their own kingdom. They do not have *chlorophyll*—the substance that gives leaves their green color. Plants use chlorophyll to change light, carbon dioxide, and water into food through the process called *photosynthesis*. Because fungi do not have chlorophyll to help make their own food, they take their nourishment from living or decaying plants or other organic things. And they do not have pollen. Instead they reproduce by creating microscopic units called *spores*.

Mushrooms are one kind of fungi. They need to distribute their spores in order to make more mushrooms, and they've evolved various ways of doing so.

Close-up on Stinkhorns

Few fungi use as delightfully disgusting a spore-spreading method as the stinkhorns. These mushrooms are found all over North America. They pop up egg-shaped from the ground and grow quickly into rods or other forms. Soon they produce a slime that smells like dog doo or roadkill.

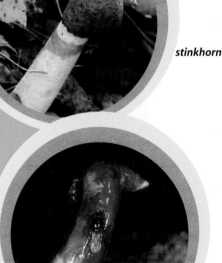

mushroom on a tree stump

stinkhorn

flies feasting on a gooey stinkhorn

Bluebottles and other flies land on top of the mushrooms to feast on the goo. The spores stick to the insects' legs or are eaten. They also contain chemicals to make the flies poop quickly. Soon after the flies leave, the spores fall off or are excreted, land on the ground, and eventually turn into new stinkhorns.

Believe it or not, some people eat stinkhorns. The "eggs" of some stinkhorn species are delicacies in China and other parts of the world. But you have to be a mushroom expert to recognize them, because they can be confused with deadly poisonous *Amanita*s. You may prefer to stick with hens' eggs instead—scrambled with chopped mushrooms from the supermarket. No danger—and no slime!

Fungi: The Good, the Bad, and the Smelly

Fungi are responsible for many strong smells. Some of these organisms are harmful, such as the ones that cause mildew and athlete's foot, a contagious infection that causes the skin to crack and itch. But others are very helpful indeed. Varieties of *Penicillium* give us the antibiotic penicillin, as well as many delicious and quite smelly cheeses, such as bleu cheese and Camembert.

grapes with bunch rot

More fungus discoveries are made every day. During a recent expedition to a Central American rain forest, a scientist named Gary Strobel noticed that a cinnamon tree was unharmed by pests. Within the tree was *Muscodor albus*, or "stinky white fungus." This fungus produces noxious gases that repel insects, bacteria, and harmful fungi. Research suggests that *Muscodor* can be used as a natural pesticide and insecticide to replace chemicals that are much more dangerous to humans.

Can the same fungus be both good and bad? You bet! In damp, humid conditions, a gray fungus, *Botrytis cinerea,* infects wine grapes and produces "bunch rot," which kills them—a smelly and nasty problem for farmers. But when drier weather follows wet weather, the same *Botrytis* can create "noble rot." It shrivels the fruit and results in an especially fine dessert wine with a sweet taste and aroma truly fit for noble men and women!

If It Smells Bad, It MIGHT Be Good for You!

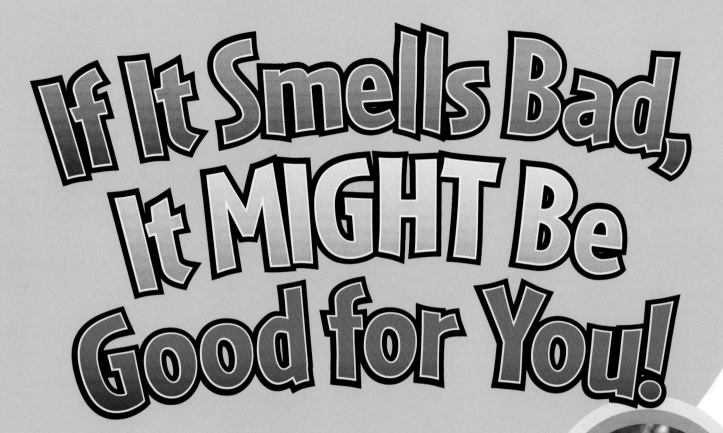

BELIEVE IT OR NOT, NOTHING WILL GET RID OF ONION BREATH!

Some malodorous plants appeal to other animals, but not to people. And some strong-smelling flora that turns off other mammals and insects are appealing to humans. Among those plants, many are not only good to eat, but are also good for you. Did anyone say "onions"?

Toothpaste. Mouthwash. Breath mints. Chewing gum. You can try them all, but none of them will ever get rid of onion breath. That's because several *sulfides*—the chemicals that give onions and garlic their famous odors—get absorbed into your lungs and linger there for hours. These chemicals can also be absorbed right through your skin. If a pregnant woman eats a lot of garlic, her newborn baby will often have garlic breath, too.

flowering garlic

onion blooms

From Bad Breath to Better Health

Onions, garlic, and other members of the allium family will make your breath reek, but they may also make you healthy. According to many scientists, the smelly sulfides seem to destroy bacteria, viruses, and other pests. They also may help you avoid or at least recover more quickly from colds, flu, and other illnesses.

Garlic can be medicinal.

The onions' leaves and the bulbs—the part we eat—stink. When cooked, onions and their relatives generally lose much of their odor. Unlike the rafflesia, onions and garlic don't use their smell to attract insect pollinators, but to repel bugs that might want to eat them. Planted among other vegetables and even some fruits, onions and garlic will even repel bugs from them—without making those foods taste oniony.

The flowers that bloom on allium plants usually don't stink, and some varieties even smell sweet. Believe it or not, the onion is related to the beautiful flowering lily. Considering all the helpful, healthful things an onion offers, it's no wonder some folks prize this stinker above its sweet-smelling relative.

CAN YOU NAME THESE ALLIUMS?

ANSWERS: a) garlic; b) scallions; c) chives; d) onions; e) leeks

Grow a Garden of Stinky Delights

Many gardeners plant flowers and herbs for their lovely fragrance. But they plant other herbs and flowers to make deer, rabbits, insects, and other garden pests go, "Ewww!" Here are some:

cleome

tomato plant

Originally from South America, the "spider-plant" has tall, extraordinary-looking pink, white, rose or violet flowers that resemble huge daddy longlegs. It's an unfussy plant that can tolerate heat and drought, plus it reseeds readily. And, of course, it stinks! Its fetid leaves have earned it the name of "skunk weed."

Cleome repels deer and other animals—and maybe you. But it's worth putting up with the smell to have these lovely blooms. Plant seeds or seedlings in well-drained soil in full sun toward the back of your garden. Then hold your nose and watch butterflies and hummingbirds come to feast.

Most people like the smell of fresh tomatoes. But how about tomato *leaves*? Rub a tomato leaf with your fingers and take a whiff. Ugh! Besides smelling bad, what are those leaves good for? Insecticide to rid your plants of juice-sucking aphids.

Try this: Finely chop one cup of the leaves and soak them in two cups of water for one full day. Strain the water into a spray bottle and add two cups of fresh water. Presto! You have a great aphid killer! But don't use the spray on plants related to tomatoes—potatoes, eggplant, or peppers—or you might give them plant diseases.

marigolds

Most people enjoy the dazzling orange, yellow, red, or white marigold blossoms. And nothing smells like a marigold—except another marigold. Bees and some people think it's a delicious fragrance. Other people—and slugs—think it reeks.

They are among the easiest flowers to grow. They aren't fussy about soil, can withstand heat, and have few insect pests. Just give them plenty of sun, and they'll make your garden smell, well, "marigold-y."

fritillaria

Also called "Crown Imperial," this plant looks beautiful but smells horrible. First, there's the skunky bulb. Bury it six inches deep in good soil during the fall, and in the spring, bell-shaped orange or yellow flowers will appear on stalks that can grow up to five feet tall.

The stinky flowers of the fritillaria attract insect pollinators—and keep rodents away from your vegetables!

rue

An aromatic herb, rue is a hearty grower that thrives in poor soil. Some people get a rash from this plant, so it's best to handle it while wearing gardening gloves. The odor is more medicinal than disgusting. It's so powerful, especially if the leaves or stems are crushed or bruised, that it makes a good pest repellent.

In the Middle Ages, people carried rue to ward off fleas and other bugs—and possibly each other!

coriander

The name for this parsley-looking herb comes from the Greek word for "bedbug," either because the seeds look buggy or because they *smell* buggy before they are ripe. The seeds are used in cooking and so are the leaves, which are also known as "cilantro." The leaves have a strong odor, too. Some people like the odor; others can't stand it. Plant coriander in a sunny spot or in a pot. Then you can decide on the smell for yourself.

chives

Like onions and garlic, chives are alliums. But, unlike onions and garlic, we don't eat chive bulbs. We eat the narrow, hollow leaves. Chives have lovely pink or purple flowers, which have no fragrance and look pretty in a garden. They also grow well in a pot on your windowsill.

Cut the leaves indoors, and you can perfume your house with their familiar onion odor. They taste great with sour cream on baked potatoes.

Gross–but Good for You

Asafoetida has been called both "food of the gods" and "devil's dung." Its name actually means "stinking resin," and its odor resembles rotten onions or sulfur. To harvest it, gardeners chop off the stems and make cuts in the roots of a very smelly, giant herb called wild fennel. The milky sap oozes out and dries into a resin. Then the plant is cut again and again until enough resin is harvested. It takes about three months to collect two pounds of this divinely smelly spice.

asafoetida pills

Used as a seasoning in ancient Rome and sometimes taken as a medicine throughout Europe, Asia, and the U.S., it has even been used as an aid to singers (supposedly to improve their voices). Today it is most often used in Indian cooking and is called "hing." When it is heated, asafoetida loses its bad odor and adds a pleasant onion flavor to food.

Try This On for Size–Uh, Smell!

Put four peeled cloves of garlic in your sock and wear them. Check your breath seven hours later. P.U.!

Making Sense of Scents

Shakespeare

William Shakespeare once wrote:

*"What's in a name?
That which we call a
rose, by any other name
would smell as sweet."*

Well, some scientists disagree with old Will. It's true that different people have different sensitivity to smells. It's also true that some aromas that we dislike (ammonia, for example) irritate the nerves in our noses.

Many animals are born with instinctive reactions to certain odors, such as squirrels avoiding fox urine. But a growing number of researchers believe that humans are taught to like or dislike smells. They believe that our reactions to odors are based on memory, experience, and assumptions.

roses

Science and Smell

Scientists conducted experiments in which people were asked to sniff two glasses of liquid that had the same exact smell—but one glass was dyed and the other was colorless. The majority of folks believed that the colored fluid smelled stronger than the clear one.

Dr. Rachel S. Herz, a psychologist at Brown University, has extensively studied smell. One of Dr. Herz's subjects told her she disliked the smell of roses because it reminded her of her mother's funeral. Dr. Herz herself enjoys the faint scent of skunk because the first time she smelled it was on a lovely, sunny day, and her mother said it was a nice odor.

Dr. Herz and Julia von Clef conducted a study in which people got to sniff various fragrances and decide whether they were pleasant or nasty. When they were told that one particular aroma was Parmesan cheese, they tended to call it yummy. But when they were informed that the *same* odor was vomit, they said it was disgusting.

In another study, thirty-six people tested two new scents, as well as several familiar ones. They initially rated the new odors as pleasant and unfamiliar. But then the people were split into groups. One entered a scented room and played a frustrating computer card game. Another group went into a second room with a different scent and read magazines. A third group played the computer game in an odorless room. After several sessions over the course of a week, the participants rated the new and familiar odors again. After playing the annoying computer game, they tended to score the pleasing new odors as nasty.

DO PARMESAN CHEESE AND VOMIT SMELL THE SAME?

These results may indicate that our response to a scent is influenced by conditions and circumstances. They also suggest that fragrances may be used to help people feel better, such as in the practice of aromatherapy. Dr. Herz says that hospitals might use an odor that a person believes is pleasant to help him or her feel better and recover more quickly.

Scientists are still debating whether or not our perception of smell is learned. One thing we do know is that you may love your perfume and your best pal may think it reeks.

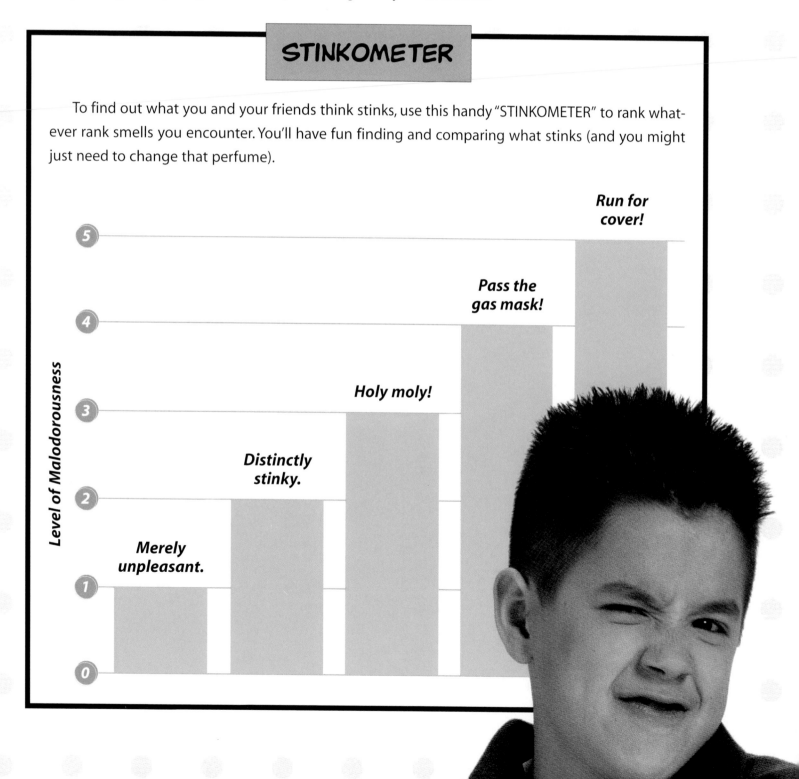

STINKOMETER

To find out what you and your friends think stinks, use this handy "STINKOMETER" to rank whatever rank smells you encounter. You'll have fun finding and comparing what stinks (and you might just need to change that perfume).

Level of Malodorousness

5
4 — Run for cover!
3 — Pass the gas mask!
2 — Holy moly!
1 — Distinctly stinky.
0 — Merely unpleasant.

Vocabulary That Reeks

Author Acknowledgments

Thanks to my husband and best critic Steve Aronson, my editor Tanya Dean
and the crew at Darby Creek Publishing, and the following experts for information:

Dr. Rachel S. Herz (Brown University)

Joyce Kaplan (Pensacola Junior College)

Louis Sorkin and David Grimaldi (American Museum of Natural History: www.amnh.com)

Duncan Butchart (African Wildlife—Wildwatch: www.wildwatch.com)

Dr. Charles Cole (Pest Network)

Lynn Butler (Plant Delights Nursery)

Bruce R. Maslin (Western Australian Department of Conservation and Land Management)

Nan Johnson (Lady Bird Johnson Wildflower Center: www.wildflower.org)

Lynn Clark (Iowa State University)

Susan Adams (NatureWorks: www.nhptv.org/natureworks/default.htm)

Bo Jensen (http://hjem.get2net.dk/bojensen)

Thomas Eisner (Cornell University)

George Pratt (Tasman Bay Roses)

Rachel Dugas (www.wingsinflight.com)

Matthew Shepherd (Xerces Society for Invertebrate Conservation: www.xerces.org)

Danielle DuCharme (Bohart Museum of Entomology: http://bohart.ucdavis.edu)

LariAnn Garner (Aroidia Research)

Dr. Michael Kuo (www.mushroomexpert.com)

Michael Wood (www.mykoweb.com)

Jeff Schalau (University of Arizona Cooperative Extension)

Dr. Susan K. Mikota (Elephant Care International: www.elephantcare.org)

The Gardener's Resource Center at the Brooklyn Botanic Garden (www.bbg.org)

The Wildlife Conservation Society (www.wcs.org/zoos)

Gigi Allianic, Farshid Mehrdadfar, and Dana Payne (Woodland Park Zoo: www.zoo.org)

Kerry Crosbie (http://asianrhinos.org.au)

Claudio Sillero (http://www.canids.org)

Marc Baldwin (www.wildlifeonline.me.uk)

Jan Dietrick (http://cincinnatizoo.org)

Don and Lillian Stokes (www.stokesbooks.com)

—A special thanks to **Paul L. Sieswerda** (New York Aquarium: www.nyaquarium.com)
for fact-checking this manuscript.

Bibliography

I read many books and articles for research. Here are several of them.

BOOKS AND ARTICLES

Benyus, Janine M. *Beastly Behaviors*. Boston: Addison-Wesley, 1992.

Downer, John. *Weird Nature*. Buffalo, NY: Firefly Books, 2002.

Edmunds, Malcolm. *Defence in Animals*. Harlow, UK: Longman, 1974.

Eisner, Thomas. *For the Love of Insects*. Cambridge, MA: The Belnap Press of Harvard University Press, 2003.

Ernst, Carl H. and George R. Zug. *Snakes in Question*. Washington, D.C.: Smithsonian Institution Press, 1996.

Halfpenny, James. *A Field Guild to Mammal Tracking in North America*. Boulder, CO: Johnson Books, 1986.

Hanson, Jeanne K. and Deane Morrison. *Of Kinkajous, Capybaras, Horned Beetles, Seladangs and the Oddest and Most Wonderful Mammals, Insects, Birds, and Plants of Our World*. New York: HarperCollins, 1991.

Herz, Rachel S. and Julia von Clef. "The influence of verbal labeling on the perception of odors: Evidence for olfactory illusions?" *Perception*: 30 (2001): 381-391.

Klots, Alexander B. and Elsie. *1001 Questions Answered about Insects*. New York: Dover Publications, 1961.

Lacey, Stephen. *Scent in Your Garden*. London: Frances Lincoln Limited, 1991.

MacDonald, Dr. David, ed. *The Encyclopedia of Animals*. New York: Facts on File, 1995.

O'Toole, Christopher. *Alien Empire: An Exploration of the Lives of Insects*. New York: HarperCollins, 1995.

Polese, Jean-Mari. *The Great Encyclopedia of Mushrooms*. Cologne, Germany: Konemann, 1999.

Preston-Mafham, Rod and Ken. *The Natural History of Insects*. Marlborough, UK: The Crowood Press, 1996.

Schaechter, Elio. *In the Company of Mushrooms*. Cambridge, MA: Harvard University Press, 1997.

Singer, Marilyn. *The Fanatic's Ecstatic Aromatic Guide to Onions, Garlic, Shallots, and Leeks*. Englewood Cliffs, NJ: Prentice-Hall, 1981.

Sleeman, Paddy. *Stoats & Weasels, Polecats & Martens*. London: Whittet Books, 1989.

Stokes, Donald and Lillian. *Stokes Nature Guides: A Guide to Animal Tracking and Behavior*. Boston: Little, Brown and Company, 1986.

Tyning, Thomas F. *Stokes Nature Guides: A Guide to Amphibians and Reptiles*. Boston: Little, Brown and Company, 1990.

Waldbauer Dr. Gilbert. *The Handy Bug Answer Book*. Detroit: Visible Ink Press, 1999.

SOURCES ON THE INTERNET
(in order of appearance in the book)

Lemurs
www.primatecenter.duke.edu/
www.brookfieldzoo.org/pagegen/htm/fix/fg/fg_body.asp?s
   Animal=Ring-tailed+lemur

Fulmars
www.colostate.edu/Depts/Entomology/courses/en570/
   papers_1998/skinner.html

Vultures
www.raptorrehab.org/new/tv.htm
www.wingmasters.net/tvulture.htm

Pelicans
www.birdchick.com/adventures/pelicans/pelicans.html

Hoatzins
www.science-frontiers.com/sf066/sf066b06.htm

Acorn worms
www.wildsingapore.com/chekjawa/text/s311.htm
www.cobscook.org/cobscook_bay/soundings/smell.htm

Stinkpot turtles
www.trentu.ca/biology/turtlewatch/stinkpot.htm

Skunks
www.dragoo.org/
www.eduscapes.com/nature/skunk/index2.htm
www.humboldt.edu/~wfw2/skunkspray.shtml

Porcupines
www.enature.com/fieldguide/showSpeciesGS.asp?cur?
   Group ID=5&searchText=porcupine&curPageNum=
   1&   recnum=MA0102

Elephants
www.elephantvoices.org/index.php?topic=how_comm
www.undp.org.vn/mlist/envirovlc/022002/post106.htm

Carrion flowers
(rafflesia, skunk cabbage, dead horse arum, etc.)
http://waynesword.palomar.edu/ww0602.htm
www.sciencenews.org/articles/20031213/bob9.asp
www.plantdelights.com/Tony/bizarre.html
www.abc.net.au/science/news/stories/s747468.htm
www.earlham.edu/~givenbe/Rafflesia/rafflesia/
   biodiv2.htm

Baobabs and Bats
http://geoimages.berkeley.edu/Geoimages/Johnson/
   Biomes/BiomesAfrica/Baobabtree.html
www.lubee.org
www.szgdocent.org/resource/ff/f-batrol.htm

Proteas
http://protea.worldonline.co.za/p52prhumi.htm

Stinkhorns
www.wildmanstevebrill.com/Mushrooms.Folder/Elegant
   %20Stinkhorn.html
http://www.fcps.k12.va.us/StratfordLandingES/Ecology/
   mpages/elegant_stinkhorn.htm

Durians
www.ecst.csuchico.edu/~durian/
www.durianpalace.com/

Ginkgoes
www.xs4all.nl/~kwanten/thetree.htm
www.scidiv.bcc.ctc.edu/rkr/ginkgo/ginkgo.html

Ailanthus
www.hort.purdue.edu/newcrop/duke_energy/Ailanthus_
   altissima.html

Stink grass
www.missouriplants.com/Grasses/Eragrostis_cilianensis_
   page.html

Asafoetida
www.botanical.com/botanical/mgmh/a/asafe070.html
www.uni-graz.at/~katzer/engl/generic_frame.html?
   Feru_ass.html
www.ibiblio.org/herbmed/eclectic/usdisp/ferula-asaf.html

Scented plants
www.millsfarmplants.co.uk/Scented_plants.htm

Deer-resistant plants
www.bbg.org/gar2/topics/sustainable/2001wi_deerresistant.
   html

About smells
www.psycport.com/showArticle.cfm?xmlFile=krt%5F2002
   %5F04%5F09%5Fknige%5F2048%2D0122%2DSCI
   %2DSIEGFRIED%2DCOLUMN%2EDA%2Exml&
   provider=Knight%20Ridder%2FTribune

Glossary

abdomen—the end section of an insect or arachnid's body; it contains the digestive system and reproductive organs. Also the area in mammals and other animals that contains the main digestive organs.

aggregation pheromone—a chemical substance given off by a group of animals, especially insects, when gathering together in one place.

allelopathy—a chemical process that a plant species uses to prevent other plants from growing too close to it.

allium—a usually strong-smelling, bulbous plant in the lily family; onions, chives, garlic, and leeks are all alliums.

anal gland—a gland located on or near an animal's rear end. See GLAND.

antenna—one of a pair of slender, movable organs on the head of an insect and other animals used for smell, taste, and touch; a feeler. Plural: **antennae.**

aposematic—having warning colors, patterns, or structures to show that an animal tastes bad or is poisonous. Noun: **aposematism.**

arachnid—a class of arthropods, including spiders, scorpions, mites, and ticks, which have eight legs and bodies divided into two sections.

arthropod—an animal with an outer shell or exoskeleton and no backbone.

bacterium—a one-celled microorganism found inside and outside animal bodies; it may be helpful, harmful, or harmless. Plural: **bacteria**.

bug—a true bug is of the order *Heteroptera*. Also, the common term for an insect or arachnid.

camouflage—hiding in plain sight by means of disguise or protective coloring.

carnivore—a flesh-eating animal. Adjective: **carnivorous**.

carrion—dead and decaying flesh.

cephalothorax—the combined head and thorax of an arachnid or other related animal.

chlorophyll—the green coloring found in plants, which helps them change sunlight, water, and carbon dioxide to food in the process called PHOTOSYNTHESIS.

crop—an enlarged pouched area in the chest of many birds where food begins to be digested.

deodorant—a substance, often scented, used to mask or destroy unpleasant odors.

diurnal—active primarily during the daytime.

elytra—the hard forewings of beetles and other insects that protect the soft hind wings.

estrus—the mating period for most female mammals, also known as "heat."

excrement—waste matter discharged from the body. Also called feces and dung.

fertilizer—a substance, such as manure or a chemical mixture, which is put into the soil to promote plant growth.

flatus—gas generated in the stomach or bowels.

flora—the plant or plant life of a period, a region, or an environment.

fungus—a spore-producing organism that lacks chlorophyll and gets nutrients from dead or living plants or animals. Plural: **fungi**.

gland—an organ or structure in or on an animal's body that secretes a substance used elsewhere in the body.

guano—the excrement of seabirds and bats.

halitosis—bad breath.

Heteroptera—a type of insect that has beaklike, sucking mouth parts and forewings that are half-hard and half-soft and thin.

hydrogen cyanide—the poisonous, usually gaseous compound that has the odor of bitter almonds.

insect—an animal with no backbone, an exoskeleton, three body sections (head, thorax, and abdomen), six legs, and usually one or two pairs of wings.

insecticide—a substance used to destroy insects.

insectivore—an animal, such as a mole, shrew, or hedgehog that feeds mainly on insects. Adjective: **insectivorous.**

invasive species—aggressive plants or animals that tend to invade or take over a habitat.

manure—livestock excrement used as fertilizer.

marsupial—any of a group of mammals, such as a kangaroo Tasmanian devil, or opossum, known for the female's ability to carry her young in a pouch on her abdomen.

mephitid—a member of the skunk family, an omnivorous mammal that can spray a pungent, offensive odor from a pair of glands on its rear end.

microbe—a microorganism, or tiny plant or animal; often a bacterium that can cause disease.

mildew—a type of fungus that produces a whitish growth on plants, cloth, paper, and other organic matter.

moda—a type of musth in which a young male elephant's secretions smell sweet, like honey or flowers.

mucus—the thick, slippery substance a body's glands and membranes produce to keep organs and other parts moist and protected.

musk—a substance with a strong, long-lasting odor that is found in the abdominal sac of the male musk deer.

mustelid—a member of a group of mammals, including weasels, stoats, minks, otters, polecats, wolverines, badgers, and ferrets that has large anal scent glands.

musth—an annual state of the male, or bull, elephant connected to the mating season and characterized by aggressive behavior and bodily secretions.

nectar—a sweet liquid given off by plants and used by bees to make honey.

nocturnal—active primarily during the night.

odorant—an odorous substance.

olfactory—of, relating to, or connected to the sense of smell.

olfactory fatigue—a condition in which one's sense of smell gets so tired that one can no longer detect a particular odor.

omnivore—an animal that eats both plants and animals. Adjective: **omnivorous**.

osmeterium—an aposematic gland on some caterpillars, especially swallowtails, that emits a disagreeable odor for defense purposes.

parasite—an organism that depends on another living being for food and shelter, but does not give anything useful in return.

pesticide—a substance used to destroy pests, especially insects.

pheromone—an airborne chemical substance produced by an animal which influences the behavior or physical development of other individuals of the same species.

photosynthesis—the process by which plants use chlorophyll to change sunlight, carbon dioxide, and water into food.

pincers—the grasping claw-like parts in the front or rear of an insect or other animal.

pollination—the process by which plants reproduce, involving the transfer of powder-like pollen from the male flower parts to the female parts.

preen gland—a gland that secretes oil that birds use to groom their feathers.

primate—a member of a group of advanced mammals, including humans, apes, monkeys, and lemurs, which can grasp things with their fingers and opposable thumbs.

receptor cell—a cell that receives and responds to a particular odor or other stimulus.

resin—a thick, clear or, colored solid or semi-solid substance formed in plant secretions.

saliva—a watery secretion from glands in an animal's mouth used to moisten food and begin digestion.

scat—an animal fecal dropping.

secretion—a moist substance released by an animal or plant, such as saliva, scent, or tears.

sphincter—a ring-like muscle surrounding a bodily opening that allows it to open and close.

spore—a microscopic reproductive cell produced by fungi, some plants, and certain microorganisms that is capable of developing into a new individual.

sulfide—a smelly organic compound characterized by a sulfur atom attached to two carbon atoms.

temporal gland—one of a pair of glands located on the side of the skull.

thorax—the middle of the three chief divisions of of an insect to which the wings are attached.

toxin—a poisonous substance.

urine—liquid waste material that is secreted by the kidneys in mammals and other animals.

venom—a poisonous secretion from an animal that is injected into prey or enemies by fangs, stingers, or other means.

vermin—any of small, common pests that are harmful and difficult to control, such as a rat, mouse, or cockroach.

Index